Genealogical Memoirs

of the

Family *of*

ROBERT BURNS

and of the

Scottish House *of* Burnes

BY THE

Rev. Charles Rogers, LL.D.

HISTORIOGRAPHER TO THE ROYAL HISTORICAL SOCIETY, FELLOW OF THE SOCIETY OF ANTIQUARIES OF SCOTLAND, FELLOW OF THE ROYAL SOCIETY OF NORTHERN ANTIQUARIES, COPENHAGEN; MEMBER OF THE HISTORICAL SOCIETY OF QUEBEC, MEMBER OF THE HISTORICAL SOCIETY OF PENNSYLVANIA, AND CORRESPONDING MEMBER OF THE HISTORICAL AND GENEALOGICAL SOCIETY OF NEW ENGLAND

HERITAGE BOOKS
2009

HERITAGE BOOKS

AN IMPRINT OF HERITAGE BOOKS, INC.

Books, CDs, and more—Worldwide

For our listing of thousands of titles see our website
at
www.HeritageBooks.com

A Facsimile Reprint
Published 2009 by
HERITAGE BOOKS, INC.
Publishing Division
100 Railroad Ave. #104
Westminster, Maryland 21157

Originally published:
London
Printed for the
Royal Historical Society
1877

International Standard Book Numbers
Paperbound: 978-0-7884-3013-8
Clothbound: 978-0-7884-7595-5

PREFACE.

OF the numerous biographers of the poet Burns, few have dilated on his lineage. Some doubtless felt that his position might not be elevated by any pedigree, however famous. Others may have been content to hold that himself being in lowly circumstances, any inquiry as to his progenitors would be useless and unprofitable. By his biographer Dr Currie he is described as "in reality a peasant."

What in respect of descent Burns really was these Memoirs will show. Remotely sprung from a landed stock, his immediate ancestors were yeomen, at first opulent, latterly the reverse. The family had produced another poet, the author of "Thrummy Cap;" but decided indications of intellectual activity did not appear in the house till subsequent to the marriage of the poet's paternal grandfather. The wife of this person was of the family of Keith of Craig, a branch of the house of Keith-Marischal. From the Keiths of Craig have sprung, among many other eminent persons, the celebrated Ambassador Keith, the Right Hon. Sir Robert Murray Keith, and Mrs Anne Keith, a considerable poetess and the accomplished friend of Sir Walter Scott. Isabella Keith, wife of Robert Burnes at Clochnahill, was mother of three sons who reached manhood. The eldest was grandfather of Sir Alexander Burnes, linguist, diplomatist, and traveller; the second had a daughter pronounced by the poet the smartest of her kin; the third was the poet's father.

The family name was originally Burnes; it has been variously spelt—Burnace, Burnice, and Burness. For a time the poet spelt it Burness; but prior to issuing proposals for the first edition of his poems in 1786, he finally changed the spelling to Burns, as the name was usually rendered in Ayrshire. Not a few descendants of the house, especially in the north of Scotland, adopt the form of Burness.

The present work is chiefly founded on Dr James Burnes' "Notes on his Name and Family," a thin duodecimo privately printed in 1851, and on entries in the parochial and other registers. Among the members of the poet's family who have afforded willing help may be named Mr Gilbert Burns, of Dublin, his nephew; Misses Agnes and Isabella Begg, of Alloway, his nieces; Mrs Everitt and Mrs Hutchinson, his grandchildren; and his relatives Mrs Adam Burnes and Lieutenant Albert Whish, both of Montrose. In many ways Mr Myers, town clerk of Montrose, Mr James Gibson of Liverpool, and Mr James M'Kie of Kilmarnock, have rendered praiseworthy and important service. Through the good offices of James Cowie, Esq., Sundridge Hall, Kent, an accurate account is for the first time presented of the circumstances under which the poet's grandfather, Robert Burnes, quitted the farm of Clochnahill, an event bearing materially on the latter history of the family. To render the genealogical narrative minute and accurate, no effort has been spared.

GRAMPIAN LODGE, FOREST HILL, S.E.,
        October 1877.

GENEALOGICAL MEMOIRS.

ETC. ETC.

THE name Burns or Burnes is probably derived from the Anglo-Saxon *Beorn*, a chief, with the affix *nes*, denoting possession. At Burnesburgh, in Yorkshire, Athelstan, in 938,[1] defeated the Danes and Scots. Burneston-juxta-Ermuldon, in Northumberland, was one of the estates left in 1391 [2] by Jacoba, wife of John de Stryvelyn. The manor of Burneston, in Derbyshire, belonging to the abbey of Welbeck, and other places so called, are named in the reigns of Henry VIII. and Elizabeth.[3] Burnestede, in Norfolk, belonged to Beatrix, Countess of Arundel, in 1440;[4] and Burneshead, in Cumberland, was the seat of a family named Burnes up to the reign of Edward I.[5]

In Domesday Book in 1050 Godric de Burnes appears as owner of wide domains in Kent.[6] In the reigns of Richard I. and John (1189-1216) are named, in connection with property in Kent, Eustace de Burnes, Roger de Burnes, and William

---

[1] Hardyng's Chronicle, Lond. 1543.

[2] Calendar. Inquisit. Post Mort., Lond. 1821, vol. iii., p. 127.

[3] Valor Ecclesiasticus, temp. Henry VIII., Lond. 1825 ; Ducatus Lancastriæ, Lond. 1827.

[4] Calendar. Inquisit. Post Mort., vol. iv., p. 197.

[5] Burn's Cumberland, Lond. 1777, vol. i., p. 124.

Ellis' Introduction to Domesday Book, vol. ii., p. 63.

de Burnes.[1] John de Burnes, *miles*, is, in a bull of Pope Nicholas IV., welcomed to Rome in 1290 as envoy of Edward I.;[2] he afterwards appears as sheriff of Kent; also in connection with various important public transactions.[3] In a charter of Edward II., William de Burnes is included among the earlier benefactors to the hospital founded by Thomas à Becket at Eastbridge, in Canterbury.[4]

The name is also at an early date to be found in Scotland "Robert del Brunhouse, tenant le Euesge de Seint Andreu del counte de Edeneburgh," is twice mentioned in connection with the oaths of allegiance tendered to Edward I.[5] *Bernes* or *Bernis*, as place-names, appear in numerous charters of the reign of Robert the Bruce.[6] To John Menteith, King Robert granted a charter of the lands of Bernis, in the thanedom of Aberluthnot and county of Kincardine.[7] These lands were afterwards known as Burnhouse of Kair, and from these it is probable that the Kincardineshire family of Burnes derived their surname. A tradition that the original name of the Burnes family was Campbell may rest upon some foundation, but the tradition is too vague to be positively affirmed. A family named Burnes certainly existed in Kincardineshire early in the sixteenth century, and this family, there is every reason to believe, obtained its name from the lands of Bernis or Burnhouse.

[1] Placitorum Abbrevatio, temp. Ric. I.

[2] Rymer's Fœdera, Lond. 1816, vol. i., part ii., p. 740.

[3] Ruding's Annals of Coinage ; Rymer's Fœdera ; Hasted, vol. i., pp. i., ii.

[4] Dugdale's Monasticon, vol. vi., p. 692.

[5] Ragman Rolls, 147.

[6] At the north-west extremity of Sanday, one of the Orkney isles, is the parish of Burness ; a lake in the island of Westray is so styled ; and there is an estate of the name on the mainland of Orkney, near Kirkwall.

[7] Robertson's Index, 17, 56.

Near Burnhouse of Kair lie the lands of Inchbreck, in the parish of Glenbervie. These lands were in 1547 granted by Sir Alexander Douglas of Glenbervie to David Stuart, in reward of his care of the granter when he lay wounded on the field of Pinkie. On the authority of the late Professor Stuart of Aberdeen, owner of Inchbreck, we learn that in 1547 the lands were rented by persons named Burnes, whose descendants continued to occupy the lands.[1]

On the 5th April 1637, "John Burnes, servitor," probably factor or chamberlain to Sir Alexander Strachan of Thornton, attached his name at Edinburgh to a deed granted by the Earl of Traquair, Treasurer of Scotland, to Alexander Straitown of that ilk.[2] The lands of Thornton are situated in Kincardineshire, in the district of Glenbervie or Inchbreck, where we obtain the first trace of the Burnes family. The name of Patrick Burness, clerk to the Presbytery of Brechin, is attached to a bond, whereby, on the 26th August 1659, John Lindsay of Edzell granted "ane hundreth merks and six bolls of oatmeal, etc." to the "Reader of Loghlie."[3]

In the parish churchyard of Glenbervie four tombstones commemorate members of the Burnes family, farmers on the Inchbreck estate. One of these, in the form of a sarcophagus, elaborately decorated, records the names of William Burnes, tenant in Bogjorgan, who died in 1715, and of the members of his family. On the upper portion of the stone are the initials W. B. and C. F., between the figure of a heart, richly sculptured. Beneath are the words, " Here under lies

[1] Dr Burnes' Notes on his Name, p. 14 ; Jervise's Memorials of Angus and the Mearns, 1861, 8vo, pp. 95-99.

[2] Dr James Burnes, who relates this fact, states that the deed was in the possession of his father.—*Notes on his Name*, p. 13.

[3] Dr Burnes' Notes on his Name, p. 17.

Burnes,   1715." Then
follow the initials I. B., W. B., I. B., R. B., with these words,
"And here lies his son, John Burnes, who departed the 10th
April 17—, being of age 3–   ." At the base is the date
of erection, "1719," engraved between sculptured cross-bones.

The wife of William Burnes, " C. F." of the inscription, was
Christian Fotheringham. Of the house of Fotheringham, the
founder proceeded to Scotland from Hungary in the train of
sainted Queen Margaret, wife of Malcolm Canmore; the
family headquarters have long been Powrie, in Forfarshire, but
some of the younger branches settled in the county of Kincardine.

The initials I. B., W. B., I. B., and R. B., on William
Burnes' tombstone, seem to denote the names of his children,
who had died young. Of these, John Burnes, who is specially
commemorated, died at or subsequent to the age of thirty.

Considerably before his death, William Burnes seems to
have surrendered his farm of Bogjorgan to his sons, William
and James. These, after some time holding that farm on a
joint lease, separated in 1705, when William remained at
Bogjorgan, and James proceeded to rent the farm of Inches,
in the same county. The inventory of the home-steading of
Bogjorgan at the time of the separation was discovered by
the late Dr Robert Chambers,[1] and, as published by him, proceeded thus:

"Ane note of the biging off Bogjorgine, belonging to William Stuart, heritor thereoff, given up be William Burnasse,
present tenant of the sd. rowm, and James Burnasse, late
possessore of the halff theroff, upon the seventainth day of
Jully, 1705 years.

[1] Life and Works of Robert Burns, edited by Robert Chambers, Edin.
1853, 8vo, 4 vols., vol. i., p. 333.

" Imp. (a ffyr) houss, consisting off thrie couplles, ffour horses, two taill postes, ane midle wall with ane post ffrom the ground, with ane rooff, two pares in the syd, with ane door bandet, locked, and bared, and with ane window off two lightes, bradet, bandet, and snecked, with ane loume, all to be sufficient.

Item, ane barne, consisting of ffyve couplles, four horses, two taill postes, ane rooff, thrie pares in the syd, with ffor door locked and bandet, and back door bared and steepled, all to be sufficient.

Item, ane byre, consisting of four couplles, two in the syd, ane rooff, with door and door cheikes bandet, all to be sufficient.

" It is declared be both parties that if ther be no other inventur ffound betwixt this and Whytsonday nixt, 1706 years, that shall be ane tr(ue) inventur off the said William Burness at his removell from the said roum. In witness . . . beffor these witnesses—Robt. Middletoun in Broombank, and David Watson in Polburn, wryter hereoff.

" R. Midletone, *Witnes.*   WILL. STUART.
" D. Watson, *Witnes and Wrytr.*   1705.
                                   "W. B."

James Burnes, farmer at Inches, son of William Burnes, tenant at Bogjorgan, married Helen, daughter of George Burnes, in Elfhill; he died without issue.

William Burnes, second in Bogjorgan, married Elspet Taylor, by whom he had a son, William, and two daughters, Christian and Elspet. Christian married James Kerr, and Elspet married William Taylor, tenant in Whitebog.

William Burnes, third in Bogjorgan, married Helen, daughter of William Thomson, merchant, Drumlithie, parish of Fordoun; he died in 1784, in his sixty-fifth year; his wife died in 1779. He had four sons, William, James, Robert, and John; and seven daughters, Jean, Janet, Margaret, Isobel, Jean, Sarah, and Mary. Of these William, James, Jean, and Janet died in infancy. Margaret married Robert Dallas, merchant, Stonehaven. Robert, the elder surviving son, settled in Stonehaven; he died there in 1816. By his wife, Anne Paul, he had a son William, who established a manufactory at Stonehaven.[1]

John Burnes, younger son of William Burnes, third in Bogjorgan, was born in 1771. After some time engaging in trade, he, in 1794, enlisted in the Angus Fencibles, and while stationed at Dumfries, became acquainted with his relative, the poet Burns. At Dumfries, in 1796, he composed his metrical tale of "Thrummy Cap," which was shown to Robert Burns shortly before his death; it was afterwards published, and passed through several editions. John Burnes served with the Angus Fencibles till the regiment was disbanded in 1799; he subsequently served in the Forfarshire Militia, remaining with this corps till it was discharged in 1815. While pursuing his last vocation, as traveller for a publishing house, he perished in a snow-storm on his way from Stonehaven to Aberdeen, on the night of the 12th January 1826.

Besides his tale of "Thrummy Cap," John Burnes published, in 1819, a volume containing "The Hermit, or the Dead come to Life," a comic dramatic tale; "Rosmond and Isabella, or the Persisting Penitent," a tragedy; "The Old Soldier," a comic drama; "Sir James the Rose," a tragedy; and "Charles Montgomery," a tragedy. He subsequently published, at Montrose, "The Recruit," an interlude in one

[1] Statement by William Burnes, manufacturer, Stonehaven, to Dr Burnes, dated 22d August 1834.

act. His various compositions were acted on the provincial stage, the author assisting in the performances.[1] He married Margaret Davidson, a native of Peterhead, without issue.

Another tombstone in Glenbervie churchyard celebrates James Burnes, tenant in Brawlinmuir, younger brother, as is believed, of William Burnes in Bogjorgan. On his tombstone James Burnes and his wife are commemorated by the following inscription:

" Here under lyes the body of James Burnes, who was tenant in Brawlinmuir, who died the 23d of January 1743, aged 87 years. Also, the body of Margaret Falconer, his spouse, who departed this life the 28th of December 1749, aged 90 years.

> "Altho' our bodys worms destroy,
> Our reins consumed be ;
> Yet in our flesh and with our eyes
> Shall our Redeemer see."

For the farm of Brawlinmuir James Burnes paid a rent equal to £300 sterling.[2] According to tradition, he was a person of great sagacity and shrewdness. He lived at a period when Highland freebooters made predatory incursions into Kincardineshire. On one occasion, when these *Kateran,* as they were called, were hovering in his neighbourhood, he adopted the precaution of concealing his money in the nave of an old cart wheel which lay in the *jaw-hole* in front of his house. The aperture being plugged up, the robbers entered and left the house without suspecting the existence of the treasure they were treading upon.[3]

[1] Dramatic Writers of Scotland, by Ralston Inglis, Glasgow, 1868, 12mo, p. 26.

[2] Dr Burnes' Notes, p. 14.

[3] Chambers's Life of Burns, Edin. 1851, p. 334.

Margaret Falconer, wife of James Burnes in Brawlinmuir, belonged to an old and noble house. Ranulph, son of Walter de Lunkyn, obtained from William the Lion, about the close of the twelfth century, the office of royal falconer, with several lands in Kincardineshire, which, on account of the owner having charge of the king's hawks, were subsequently designated Halkerton. By the family was assumed the name of Falconer. Sir Alexander Falconer of Halkerton, a zealous adherent of Charles I., was by that monarch appointed a senator of the College of Justice, and was in 1647 raised to the peerage as Lord Falconer of Halkerton. He is now represented by Francis Alexander Keith Falconer, eighth Earl of Kintore.

Besides William and James Burnes, commemorated in Glenbervie churchyard, were two other brothers, one of whom, Colonel John Burnes, is mentioned in the Act of 1690, for " rescinding the forefaultures and fynes since the year 1665,"[1] but of whom nothing further is known. The other, Robert, settled at Benholm, Kincardineshire; his son Robert, a solicitor in Stonehaven, married Isabel Meldrum, by whom he had a son, Robert, who also followed the legal profession, and was latterly sheriff-substitute of Kincardineshire. He married Anne Cushnie.

By his wife, Margaret Falconer, James Burnes, farmer at Brawlinmuir, had five sons, William, Robert, George, James, and Thomas, and two daughters, Elspeth and Christian. Elspeth, the elder daughter, married —— Gavin, farmer, Drumlithiè, in the parish of Fordoun; Christian, the younger daughter, married —— Crabbie, farmer, Craigniston. Thomas, the youngest son, born 1705, died 8th June 1734; his only

[1] Acta Parl. Scot., ix. 166.

child, Margaret, died 24th March 1741, aged eight years.[1] William, the eldest son, succeeded his father as tacksman of Brawlinmuir. He married, with issue, but his children seem to have died young or unmarried.

James Burnes, fourth son of James Burnes and Margaret Falconer, was born in 1690, and died 3d April 1778, aged eighty-eight. He rented the farm of Hawkhill of Glenbervie, but on the death of his eldest brother William, obtained the lease of Brawlinmuir. He married, first, —— Christie, by whom he had four sons, James, Thomas, William (first), and William (second), and two daughters, Margaret and Catherine. He married, secondly, Catherine Beattie, a relative of Professor James Beattie (author of " The Minstrel"), by whom he had two sons, David and George. The latter died 16th October 1769, in his twenty-eighth year.

Margaret, elder daughter of James Burnes and —— Christie, was baptized 10th August 1722; Catherine, younger daughter, was baptized 3d May 1726. James, the eldest son, was baptized 29th March 1724; he rented, first, the farm of Auchtochter, in the parish of Fordoun, and latterly the farm of Higham, near Montrose. Thomas, the second son, baptized 11th February 1729, was many years employed as a gardener in England; he returned to Scotland, where he died about 1804. William (first), baptized 12th July 1731, died in infancy; William [2] (second), baptized 12th October 1735,[3] settled in Montrose, where he held office in the excise.

David, one of the two sons of James Burnes by Catherine Beattie, his second wife, succeeded his father as tacksman of

---

[1] Tombstone inscription in Glenbervie churchyard.

[2] William adopted the double s in spelling his name.—*Burnes' Notes*, p. 18.

[3] These dates of baptism have been extracted from the Parish Register of Glenbervie.

Brawlinmuir; latterly he removed to the large farm of Boghead of Kintore, where he died prior to 1830. He married, and had issue five sons and five daughters. Catherine Beattie, the eldest daughter, married Archibald Falconer, by whom she had seven sons, David, Robert, William, John (solicitor in Stonehaven), George, Archibald, and Alexander, and four daughters, Catherine, Margaret, Jane, and Isabel. Jean, the second daughter, married —— Reith, farmer, Tipperty, parish of Fordoun, by whom she had three sons, David, John, and James, and four daughters, Catherine, Jane, Margaret, and Christian. Margaret, the third daughter, married —— Ley, farmer, Knockback, by whom she had two sons, David and James, and three daughters, Jane, Margaret, and Mary. Isabel, fourth daughter, married William Urquhart. Mary, fifth and youngest daughter, married George Brown, builder, Kintore.

James Burnes, eldest son of David Burnes, farmer, Boghead of Kintore, rented the East Mains of Barras, in the parish of Kinneff; he married, with issue five sons, William, David, Alexander, John, and James, and four daughters, Catherine, Isabel, Margaret, and Helen. George, the second son, succeeded his father in the lease of Boghead of Kintore. David, third son, rented first the farm of Milltimber, and afterwards that of Knockquharn, in the district of Kintore. He married —— Smith, Kintore, by whom he had two sons, William and James.

Alexander, fourth son of David Burnes, farmer, Boghead, was a merchant-burgess of Aberdeen. He purchased the estate of Mastrick, Aberdeenshire. By his wife, Elizabeth Smith, he had a son, John, who died in childhood about 1840; also a daughter, Elizabeth Smith. Born in 1823, she married, in 1842, John Stuart, advocate, Aberdeen, and secretary of the Spalding Club. An accomplished antiquary, Mr Stuart was in 1854 appointed one of the official searchers in the Register House, Edinburgh; he was in 1873 promoted as principal keeper of the register of deeds. He died at Ambleside on the 19th July 1877, in his sixty-fourth year. The degree of LL.D. was in 1866 conferred on him by the University of Aberdeen, in recognition of his literary eminence. Of his numerous publications relating to Scottish history and antiquities, the best known is his "Sculptured Stones of Scotland," a work in two folio volumes. Dr Stuart was twice married. His first wife, Elizabeth Burnes, died on the 1st March 1848; she had a son, Robert, who died in September 1846, aged two years; also two daughters. Mary, the elder daughter, is unmarried; Jane Gordon, the second daughter, born January 1847, married in 1867 the Rev. John Woodward, of St Mary's Episcopal Church, Montrose, with issue, two sons, who died in childhood, and two daughters.

John, youngest son of David Burnes, farmer, Boghead, was a merchant in Aberdeen; he died unmarried.

George Burnes, third son of James Burnes, farmer in Brawlinmuir, rented the farm of Elfhill, in the parish of Fetteresso. He married, and had five sons and five daughters. James, the eldest son, was baptized 26th May 1729; Robert, the second son, 2d July 1730; John, the third son, 3d June 1733; George, fourth son, 22d June 1746; William, fifth son, 17th September 1749. Christian, the eldest daughter, was baptized 25th May 1735; Elizabeth, second daughter, 27th June 1737; Anne, third daughter, 6th May 1739; Jean, fourth daughter, 23d April 1744; and Helen, fifth and youngest daughter, 5th April 1747.[1] Several members of the family settled in London.

James, eldest son of George Burnes, farmer, Elfhill, succeeded to his father's lease, but latterly rented the farm of Midtoun of Barras, parish of Kinneff. He married, with issue three sons, George, Hugh, and James, and six daughters, Mary, Magdalene, Anne, Charlotte, Margaret, and Catherine. Mary, the eldest daughter, married William Fotheringham, farmer, Dubton, Glen of Cowton; Magdalene, second daughter, married Alexander Mollison, farmer, Mergie ; Anne, third daughter, married John Edward; Charlotte, fourth daughter, married David Taylor, farmer, Colliston; Margaret, fifth daughter, married Thomas Mitchell, Chapel of Barras ; and Catherine, sixth daughter, married Andrew Duthie, farmer, Bog of Glaslaw.

Hugh, second son of James Burnes, settled in London. James, the third son, succeeded his father in the lease of Midtoun of Barras; he afterwards rented the farm of Cloak of Hilton, parish of Kinneff. He married, and had five sons, Hugh, David, John, Robert, and James, and three daughters, Elizabeth, Catherine, and Isabel.

Robert Burnes, second son of James Burnes, Brawlinmuir, by his wife, Margaret Falconer, rented the farm of Kinmonth in Glenbervie, from which he removed to the more considerable farm of Clochnahill, in Dunnottar. In conjunction with the neighbouring farmers, he built a school at Clochnahill, and aided in supporting a teacher. He married Isabella Keith, of the family of Keith of Craig, by whom he had four sons and six daughters. Margaret, the eldest daughter, born 1723, married Archibald Walker at Crawton, with issue,

[1] Parish Register of Fetteresso.

James Walker, farmer in Gallowton, Dunnottar, who married and had a son, Alexander, iron merchant, Aberdeen, and a daughter, Isobel, who married James Knox in Stonehaven.

Elspet, second daughter of Robert Burnes, was baptized on the 18th August 1725. She married John Caird, farmer, Denside of Dunnottar, who is named in a letter of the poet to Mr James Burnes of Montrose, dated 21st June 1783, as a correspondent of his brother Gilbert. Of the marriage of John Caird and Elspet Burnes was born a daughter, Anne, who married Henry Watson, with issue two sons, James and Henry, and two daughters, Mary and Elspet. Also a son, Robert Caird, who married Margaret Melvin, Stonehaven, with issue a son and three daughters. The son, John, married Margaret Henderson, and settled in the parish of Markinch, Fifeshire. Of the daughters, Jean married James Sheritt, Aberdeen; Mary married George Smith of Stonehaven, who settled in London; and Margaret married James Watson, Aberdeen.

Jean, third daughter of Robert Burnes, baptized 24th May 1727, married John Burnes, sub-tenant at Bogjorgan; she died at Fetteresso without issue. Isobel, fourth daughter, baptized 18th August 1730, married in 1770 William Brand, dyer, Auchinblae, with issue a son James, who had four sons, Charles, who married Margaret Falconer; David, who married Jane Falconer; and William and James. Mary, the fifth daughter, baptized 26th October 1732, died unmarried; The sixth daughter, whose name is unknown, died in infancy.

James Burnes, eldest son of Robert Burnes and Isabella Keith, was born in 1717. Trained to merchandise, he in 1732 settled at Montrose. Of that burgh he became a burgess on the 11th September 1751, and was elected town councillor on the 26th September 1753. Esteemed for his piety and intelligence, he was ordained an elder of the parish church. He died on the 17th July 1761, at the age of forty-four. He married, in 1745, Margaret Grub (died at Bervie about 1795), by whom he had three sons and three daughters. One son and two daughters died young. Elizabeth, the only surviving daughter, married, 8th January 1768, George Hudson,[1] merchant, Bervie, and afterwards provost of that burgh, by whom she had three sons and eight daughters. Of these, two sons, George and William, and four daughters, Elizabeth, Margaret (first), Margaret (second), and Sarah Anne, died unmarried or without issue. John, the eldest son, married Jean Forster; Christian married A. Guthrie; Anne married J. Pirie, without issue; Elizabeth married Dr Douglas, surgeon, Elie; and Sarah married Dr Davidson, physician, Edinburgh.

David, eldest son of James Burnes and Margaret Grub, born 30th July 1749, married, December 1777, Jean M'Bean, by whom he had a son, Thomas, baptized 30th July 1783; also two daughters, Margaret, born 5th March 1780, and Jean, born 30th August 1781.[2]

James Burnes, second surviving son of James Burnes of Montrose, was born on the 24th December 1750. After some years holding office as schoolmaster at Montrose, he studied law, and became a solicitor.[3] With the poet he

[1] George Hudson was of English descent, his father and grandfather having come to Montrose in 1745 with Lord Robert Manners' regiment. His father married Elizabeth, daughter of William Carnegie, convener of the incorporated trades at Montrose—*Dr Burnes' Notes*, p. 35.

[2] Montrose Baptismal Register.

[3] On the death of his father, James Burnes some time resided with his uncle William, and in deference to his wish adopted the double s in spelling his name. He afterwards resumed the older form.

maintained a friendly correspondence, received a friendly visit from him in 1787, and on his premature death offered to aid in the upbringing of his children. He died at Montrose on the 12th June 1837, aged eighty-seven; his remains were deposited near those of his father, in the old burgh church-yard. He married, 6th January 1777, Anne, daughter of John Greig of Montrose, by his wife, Jean, daughter of Robert Watson of Sheilhill, Forfarshire; she was born 16th July 1749, and died 12th February 1796.

By his wife, Anne Greig, James Burnes was father of four sons and four daughters. Anne, the eldest daughter, born 16th April 1783, died in 1785; Christian, second daughter, born 15th April 1785, died in 1815 unmarried; Elizabeth, third daughter, died in 1818 unmarried; Sarah, fourth daughter, died unmarried in 1814. John, the eldest son, died in infancy in 1779; George, third son, born 30th September 1781, died in 1801; and Robert, youngest son, died in 1790.

James Burnes, second son of James Burnes and Anne Greig, was born on the 1st April 1780.[1] Articled to his father, he studied law and became a solicitor. As Dean of the Guildry incorporation, he entered the town council on the 11th December 1817, and, on the 23d September 1818, was elected chief magistrate. After an interval of four years, he was re-elected provost in September 1824; he resigned office on the 2d February 1825, when he was appointed joint town-clerk. He evinced a deep interest in municipal affairs, and having early exposed the abuses of the close burgh system, he has been described as the father of Scottish burghal reform. A zealous agriculturist, he was appointed a J.P. for Forfarshire, in recognition of his public services.

[1] Montrose Parish Reg.

He latterly resided at Brunton Place, Edinburgh, where he died on the 15th February 1852, at the age of seventy-two. His remains were deposited in Dalry cemetery, near Edinburgh, where he is commemorated on a family monument.

Provost James Burnes married, 22d April 1800, Elizabeth, sixth daughter of Adam Glegg, merchant burgess of Montrose, and provost of that burgh; she was born 5th April 1779, and died at Edinburgh on the 25th February 1851. The family of Glegg, Gleig, or Glyge, is traditionally of French origin. Adam Glegg, the first member of the family of whom we have any authentic record, was, with the members of his family, commemorated in the church of Marykirk, Kincardineshire, on a tombstone bearing the following epitaph:

"Heir lyes Adam Glyge, smith in the hill . . . Morphye, some tyme howsband to Isobel Low, who departed the 10 of Awgwst. Adam Gle . . . died in Apil 1698, aged 86. John Gleig died May 15, 1737, aged 83. Isobel Gleig died March 4th, 1761, aged 78."

John Gleig, named in the epitaph, was grandfather of Provost Adam Glegg of Montrose, who was born in 1731, and died at London on the 1st June 1807. Provost Glegg married his cousin-german, Anne (born 8th November 1738, died 22d December 1811), daughter of John Smith, provost of Brechin, by his wife, Christian Colvin, one of the three co-heiresses of Alexander Colvin, burgess of Montrose, by his wife, Christian Ramsay, descended from the old family of Ramsay of Balmain. Provost Glegg is mentioned by Boswell in his "Tour," as having conducted him and Dr Samuel Johnson to the Episcopal chapel at Montrose.

Among the descendants of Adam Glegg, blacksmith at

Marykirk, were the Right Rev. George Gleig, LL.D., Bishop of Brechin, and Primus of the Scottish Episcopal Church, who died at Stirling on the 9th March 1840, aged eighty-seven ; and his cousin, the Rev. George Gleig, minister of Arbroath, who died 19th June 1835, aged seventy-eight. Their fathers were both blacksmiths, the bishop's father pursuing his calling at Boghall, parish of Arbuthnot.

Of the marriage of James Burnes, provost of Montrose, and Elizabeth Glegg, were born nine sons and six daughters. Anne, the eldest daughter, born February 1801, and Margaret, died in infancy. Anne, second of the name, born at Montrose 17th August 1808, married, 6th April 1833, at Bhooj, in India, Captain William Ward, who died at Tanna, near Bombay, 9th July 1845, without issue. Elizabeth Burnes, born at Montrose 23d August 1809, married at Bombay, 3d March 1831, Lieutenant-General Richard Whish, son of the Rev. Richard Whish, rector of Northwold, Norfolk, and brother of Sir W. S. Whish, K.C.B., who commanded at Moultan. He died at Clifton, 10th November 1854.

Of the marriage of Lieutenant-General Richard Whish and Elizabeth Burnes [1] were born five sons and six daughters. Frederick Alexander, the eldest son, born at Ahmedabad 27th July 1833, died at Paunchgunny, India, in August 1872, a retired captain of the Royal Artillery. Albert William, second son, was born at Clifton 11th July 1843. He is a lieutenant in the Royal Navy, and holds office as Inspecting Officer of the coast-guard, Montrose. He married, 30th October 1873, Louisa Emily, third daughter of the late Captain Charles Forbes, of the 17th Regiment, and widow of Captain T. M. Hewett, by whom he has three sons, Albert Forbes,

---

[1] Mrs Elizabeth Whish, *née* Burnes, now resides at Folkestone.

born 3d January 1875; Cyril Beresford, born 3d March 1876; and Hugh Dudley, born 7th July 1877.

Arthur Richard Lewis, third son of Lieutenant-General Whish and Elizabeth Burnes, was born at Clifton on the 1st March 1847; he is manager of the National Provincial Bank of England, Lincoln's Inn. In 1867 he married Agnes Cook, by whom he has two daughters, Evelyn and Ada Margaret. Ernest Burnes, the fourth son, born at Clifton 12th September 1848, rents a grazing farm at Buenos Ayres. Cecil Holland, the youngest son, born at Clifton 9th March 1850, is a lieutenant in the Royal Navy, and is now serving on board H.M.S. "Agincourt," in the Mediterranean.

Matilda Emily, eldest daughter of Lieutenant-General Whish and Elizabeth Burnes, was born at Clifton on the 29th April 1835; she married, at Clifton, in August 1856, the Rev. Augustus Cooper, Upper Norwood, and has two children, Mabel and Augustus. Eliza Jane, second daughter, born at Clifton 31st May 1836, married her cousin, Major Edward Burnes Holland, by whom she had a son, Alexander, and a daughter, Constance. Flora Thornborough, third daughter, born at Clifton 11th January 1839, married in 1859 Major George Eales, of the 25th Native Infantry, Bombay, by whom she had a son, Lionel, and a daughter, Maud. Major Eales died in March 1874, on his passage home from India. Annette Isabella, fourth daughter, born at Boulogne-sur-Mer 21st July 1841; Clara Salter, fifth daughter, born at Clifton 19th October 1844; and Kathleen White, sixth daughter, born at Clifton 24th January 1852, are unmarried.

Jane Glegg Burnes, fourth daughter of James Burnes and Elizabeth Glegg, was born at Montrose on the 11th October 1810. She married, on the 11th July 1833, at Ahmedabad,

India, Lieutenant-Colonel James Holland, quartermaster-general of the Bombay Army. Colonel Holland retired from active service on the 14th February 1857; he now resides at the Park, Upper Norwood. By his wife, Jane Glegg Burnes, he is father of three sons and a daughter. Trevenon James Holland, the eldest son, was born at Bombay on the 31st May 1834. In 1851 he procured a commission in the Indian Army, and became assistant quartermaster-general at Bombay. On the 2d June 1869, he was for distinguished service nominated Military Companion of the Order of the Bath. Retiring from the army, 1st August 1871, with the rank of colonel, he holds office as manager of the Palace Hotel. He married in India Margaret Nicholson, by whom he has four daughters.

Edward Burnes Holland, second son of Colonel James Holland by his wife Jane G. Burnes, was born at Belgaum, India, on the 20th March 1836. In November 1850 he obtained by public competition at Cheltenham College the commission in the Indian Army awarded by Lieutenant-General Sir James Lushington, G.C.B. He became major of the Royal Engineers, and died at Bombay in March 1874. He married at Clifton, in 1858, his cousin, Eliza Jane Whish, by whom he had a son and daughter.[1]

Charles Wroughton Del Hoste Holland, third son of Colonel James Holland, was born at Bombay on the 20th January 1845. A stockbroker in London, he resides at Upper Norwood. He married, 25th February 1875, Margaret Riach, by whom he has a son.

Cecilia Agnes Holland, only daughter of Colonel James Holland and Jane G. Burnes, was born at Bombay on the

[1] See *supra*.

20th December 1846. She married, 3d January 1870, Dalton Hardy, stockbroker, London, by whom she has a son and two daughters.

Cecilia, sixth and youngest daughter of Provost James Burnes, was born at Montrose on the 10th November 1815. She married, on the 12th November 1839, at Bhooj, in India, Captain John Philip Major, 11th Bombay Native Infantry, and died at Bombay on the 16th October 1840, eight days after her husband, who died off Gogo, in the Gulf of Cambay, 8th October 1840. Captain and Mrs Major left a son, Francis Ward Major, born at Ahmedabad 12th August 1840. Having joined the Indian Army, he is now a captain in the Bombay Staff Corps, serving on the Mysore Revenue Survey. He married, 6th June 1863, Adelaide, second daughter of the late Captain Charles Forbes, of the 17th Regiment, by whom he has two sons, Francis Forbes, born 23d December 1867, and Philip Charles, born 11th May 1873, and two daughters, Adelaide Louisa, born 21st July 1864, and Violet, born 24th October 1866.

Of nine sons born to Provost James Burnes by his wife Elizabeth Glegg, Robert, born 26th July 1803, William Maule, Edward Phillips, and George Patrick, died young.

James Burnes, eldest son, was born at Montrose on the 12th February 1801. Educated to the medical profession at the University of Edinburgh and in Guy's and St Thomas' Hospitals, London, he in 1821 obtained a surgeon's commission in the East India Company's service. Distinguished as a linguist, he was permitted to explore the countries on the Bombay north-west frontier, and his account of the southernmost of the Rajpootanah states, and of the vast dreary tract between Goozerat and the Indus, was much valued. After holding different subordinate offices, he was posted in February 1823 to the 18th Native Infantry, stationed at Bombay. In 1824 he was, after a competition in the native language, appointed surgeon to the Residency at Cutch. In 1827 his professional services were at Hyderabad rendered to the Ameer of Scinde, by whom they were highly appreciated. His "Narrative of the Court of Scinde," published in 1829, contributed to his literary reputation. On sick leave he returned to Britain in 1834, when the University of Glasgow conferred upon him the degree of LL.D., and the Royal Society elected him a Fellow. From William IV. he received the honour of Guelphic knighthood. At Edinburgh he was entertained at a public banquet, and on the occasion presented with a silver vase with a commendatory inscription. He improved his three years' furlough by preparing a work on the history of the Knights Templars, which was published in 1840. In December 1837 he returned to Bombay, when he was appointed surgeon to the garrison. In 1841 he was elected secretary to the Medical Board, and in 1846 was promoted as superintending surgeon. With the rank of physician-general he was in 1847 transferred to the Poonah division. In 1848 he obtained a seat at the Medical Board. After a service of twenty-eight years, he in July 1849 retired from his professional duties in India. Before leaving Bombay he received complimentary addresses from various public bodies to which he had been helpful. He had officiated as Grand Master of the Freemason lodges of Western India, and on his departure the brethren presented him with several splendid gifts, and founded in his honour four medals, of which one was to be competed for in the academy of Montrose. On his return to Britain, Dr Burnes occupied a portion of his time in preparing materials for a history of his house, which in a thin duodecimo he printed, for private circulation, under the title of "Notes on his Name and Family." Edinburgh, 1851. He was J.P. for the counties of Middlesex and Forfar. He died at Manchester on the 19th September 1862, and his remains were deposited at Swindon Church, near Cheltenham.

Dr James Burnes married, first, on the 28th March 1829, at St Thomas' Church, Bombay, Sophia, second daughter of Major-General Sir George Holmes, K.C.B., by whom he had seven sons and two daughters. He married, secondly, on the 17th June 1862, at St Mary Abbot's, Kensington, Esther Price, daughter of a landowner in Wales. She resides at 40 Ladbrook Square, Kensington.

Sophia Holmes, elder daughter of Dr James Burnes, born at Bhooj 6th September 1832, died there on the 1st February 1833. Isabella Cecilia Holmes, the younger daughter, born at Edinburgh on the 4th February 1835, died there 24th May 1835, her remains being deposited in the Canongate churchyard.

George James Holmes Burnes, eldest son of Dr James Burnes, born at Bhooj on the 9th December 1829, obtained a commission in the 1st Bombay Fusiliers; he received a medal and two clasps for the Punjab, Moultan, and Guzerat. After a lengthened captivity, consequent on his efforts to save a child from the violence of the mutineers, he was cruelly murdered at Lucknow on the 19th November 1857. In the vestibule of the parish church, Montrose, a monumental tablet, erected by his brother officers, commemorates his valour.

Fitz-James Holmes Burnes, second son of Dr James Burnes, was born at Bhooj on the 6th September 1831.

Entering the 33d Regiment, Madras Native Infantry, he has attained professional advancement.

Holland Ward Holmes Burnes, third son of Dr James Burnes, was born at Bhooj on the 15th September 1833. Entering the Indian Navy, he died at Calcutta in 1873, when in command of the Feroze, the yacht of the governor-general.

Hamilton Farquhar Holmes Burnes, fourth son of Dr James Burnes, was born at Edinburgh on the 27th November 1836. He entered the army in 1855, and attained the rank of captain. He retired 14th November 1868, and is since deceased.

Dalhousie Holmes Burnes, fifth son of Dr James Burnes, was born at Bombay on the 5th April 1839. He became an officer of engineers, and died unmarried in 1872.

Sidney Holmes Burnes, sixth son of Dr James Burnes, was born at Bombay on the 13th August 1841. He died at London in 1871.

Alexander Holmes Burnes, youngest son of Dr James Burnes, was born at Bombay on the 11th April 1843. He entered the Bombay Army in 1860, and retired 14th September 1867.

Adam Burnes, second surviving son of James Burnes, Provost of Montrose, was born on the 19th February 1802. He was many years a solicitor in Montrose, where he died, 15th November 1872. He married, first, on the 3d September 1827, Horatia, daughter of Harry Gordon, Esq., who died November 2d, 1834; secondly, 18th June 1838, Isabella, daughter of William Scott, Esq., who survives.

By his first wife Adam Burnes had two sons, Adam and Alexander Horatio. Adam, the elder son, born 12th June 1832, emigrated to Australia; he became manager of the Colonial Bank at Melbourne. He subsequently resided in

New Zealand, and died at Sydney, N.S.W., on the 9th June 1876. He married, and had six sons, Adam William Gray, James Henry, Napier Anderson, Alexander Plunkett, Ernest Blair, George Douglas Inglis Scott, and a daughter, Mary Inglis.

Alexander Horatio, younger son of Adam Burnes by his first wife, was born 19th October 1834. He married Mary Jane Harris, by whom he has a daughter, Adamina Horatia, born October 1872. He emigrated to New Zealand, where he now resides.

By his second wife Adam Burnes had a son, James, born 24th May 1844, died 30th April 1873; also a daughter, Annie Eliza Glegg, born 15th September 1842, married, 16th May 1866, John Smythe M'Cay, solicitor, Londonderry. She has a son, Norman Henry Burnes.

Alexander Burnes, third surviving son of Provost James Burnes, was born at Montrose on the 16th May 1805. After greatly distinguishing himself at the Montrose Academy, he obtained a cadetship in the Indian Army. He arrived at Bombay on the 31st October 1821. In December 1822 he was appointed interpreter in Hindostanee to the First Extra Battalion at Surat, and soon afterwards he was employed by the judges of the Suddur Adawlut to translate the Persian documents of that court. His regiment, the 21st Native Infantry, having early in 1825 been sent to Bhooj, he accompanied it, and during the disturbances at Cutch, in April of that year, he was appointed quartermaster of brigade. A report on the statistics of Wagur, which he drew up and presented to Government in January 1827, was much commended, and acknowledged by a considerable donative. A memoir on the eastern branch of the delta of the Indus, which he published in 1828, was much approved by the authorities. On the 18th March 1828, he was appointed assistant quarter-master-general to the army. In September 1829, along with Major Holland, he assisted the political agent at Cutch in conducting a survey of the north-west frontier, an account of which he afterwards despatched to the Royal Geographical Society. In 1830 he conveyed a gift of dray horses from William IV. to Runjeet Singh, ruler of Lahore, using the occasion, as instructed, to procure more accurate details respecting the geography of the Indus. On his journey he proceeded from a port in Cutch, and to give colour as to the deviation from the ordinary route, carried with him presents to the ameers of Scinde. He completed a survey of the whole Indian delta.

Under sanction of Lord William Bentinck, Governor-General, Lieutenant Alexander Burnes conducted in 1832 an expedition into Central Asia. Returning to Bombay on the 18th January 1833, he received the thanks of the Governor-General ; and being authorised to bear his own despatches to England, he experienced a cordial reception at the India House. His " Travels in Bokhara " were published at London early in 1834; the work commanded a large sale, and was translated into French and German. Remaining in Britain for eighteen months, he received various public honours, besides being admitted a Fellow of the Royal Society. Returning to India in 1835 with the rank of captain, he was in October despatched on an important mission to Hyderabad, in Scinde. In November 1836 he was entrusted with a mission to Dost Mohammed, the ruler of Afghanistan, with a view of entering into commercial relations with him; he reached Cabool on the 20th September 1837. Meanwhile Mohammed, Shah of Persia, had besieged Herat with an army of 60,000

men, and the Indian Government began to apprehend that
Persia and Russia might unite their forces with those of
Afghanistan to make an attack on the Indian empire.
From Herat the Persians were forced to retreat, but Captain
Burnes requested Dost Mohammed to dismiss the Russian
agent Vicovitch from his court. This he refused to do, and
on the contrary dismissed Captain Burnes. Repairing to the
Governor-General at Simla, Captain Burnes was knighted
and promoted as lieutenant-colonel. From Scinde he proceeded to Beloochistan on a political mission, which proved
unsuccessful. When Shah Shoojah was restored to the throne
of Cabool, he was, in September 1839, appointed political
resident at that capital, with a salary of £3000. He remained
at Cabool not without a sense of insecurity, and on the out-
break of an insurrection for restoring Dost Mohammed, he
was set upon, and along with his brother Charles and seven
other officers, cruelly murdered. This sad event took place
on the 2d November 1841. Sir Alexander Burnes died unmarried at the age of thirty-six. In 1842, his work entitled
" Cabool; being a Narrative of a Journey to and Residence
in that City in the years 1836-7-8," was published at London.

Possessed of a deep sagacity and marvellous powers of
observation, Sir Alexander Burnes would, with a prolonged
career, have been eminently serviceable to the Government
of India. He opened up the Indus, and extended his re-
searches to the shores of the Oxus, the ruins of Samarcand,
and other territories which became the scenes of important
events. A brief memoir of his life, published by Dr George
Buist in the columns of the *Bombay Times* newspaper, is re-
produced by his brother, Dr James Burnes, in his " Notes on
his Name and Family."

David Burnes, fourth surviving son of Provost James Burnes, was born at Montrose on the 6th September 1806. Having studied medicine and passed M.D., he in 1826 entered the Royal Navy as surgeon. For several years he served on board the "Asia" on the Mediterranean station, to the entire satisfaction of his superiors, but was in 1835 obliged to quit the service consequent on broken health. He subsequently became a practitioner in London, but from an enfeebled constitution he was unable to carry out his profession. Retiring to Montrose, he there died on the 2d February 1849. He married, 20th October 1838, Harriet, second daughter of Alexander Anderson, M.D., surgeon R.N., by whom he had a son and daughter. The son, James Anderson Burnes, born 30th January 1845, is a banker at Calcutta; on the 14th December 1875, he married Emma, only daughter of the Rev. Dr Jarbo, chaplain of St James. The daughter, Charlotte Elizabeth, born 30th October 1842, resides at Bishop's Waltham, unmarried. The wife of Dr Burnes died 5th May 1873.

Charles Burnes, youngest son of James Burnes, Provost of Montrose, was born on the 12th January 1812. Lieutenant in the 17th Regiment, Bombay Native Infantry, he was murdered at Cabool, along with his elder brother, Sir Alexander Burnes, on the 2d November 1841; he died unmarried.

Of the younger sons of Robert Burnes, tacksman of Clochnahill, by his wife, Isabella Keith, George, the youngest, baptized on the 9th April 1729, died young.[1] Robert, the second son, born in 1719, was long employed as a gardener in England. Returning to Scotland at an advanced age, he died at the house of his nephew, the poet, on the 3d January

[1] Baptismal Register of Dunnottar.

1789. He was father of two sons and a daughter. John, the elder son, died young. William, the younger son, died in 1850, at an advanced age. Both were unmarried. Frances, the only daughter, was remarkable for her acuteness, and was characterised by her relative, the poet, as the smartest of his kin. She married Adam Armour, builder, Mauchline, brother of the poet's wife, and had two sons. Robert Armour, the elder son, carried on his father's business; he died in 1854. By his wife, Jean Wallace, he had several children. William, the younger son, inherited his mother's talents; and through his father's brother, Robert Armour, became opulent. He died at London about the year 1859.

William Burnes, third son of Robert Burnes and Isabella Keith, was born at Clochnahill on the 11th November 1721.[1] Along with his brother Robert he assisted his father on the farm. But the family were ruined by the terrible winter and spring of 1740, when a general scarcity supervened. The frost, which set in early, continued to the end of April, no seed being sown till May. The ridges were then formed high in the centre, as a protection against moisture; and the frost having penetrated far into the soil, and the season being advanced, the sunny side of the ridge was ploughed first, and the other side only when the thaw was complete. Consequent on this procedure, and the continuance of rough and unseasonable weather, the crop was stunted, and almost useless. In Kincardineshire many tenant-farmers were reduced to absolute poverty. Several farms in the cold district of Clochnahill were, some years subsequent to 1740, left without cultivation.

Robert Burnes, and his sons William and Robert, aban-

---

[1] Family Bible of William Burnes.

doned Clochnahill farm, not, as has been alleged by several of the poet's biographers, on account of the lease being granted to another, but solely in consequence of the storm of 1740. This information we have derived from Mr Cowie of Sundridge Hall, Kent, who long resided in the district, where his grandfather rented a farm, and to whom the local tradition was confirmed by Mrs Begg, the poet's sister, who said her father, William Burnes, often alluded to the terrible winter of 1740 as causing the family impoverishment.

When Clochnahill farm was abandoned, probably at the close of 1740, Robert Burnes retired, with his three unmarried daughters, to the cottage of Denside, in the same parish, while his sons, Robert and William, were compelled to proceed elsewhere in quest of employment.[1] They journeyed southward. In a letter to Mrs Dunlop, Gilbert Burns writes: "I have often heard my father describe his anguish of mind when they parted on the top of a hill, on the confines of their native place, each going off his several way in search of new adventures, and scarcely knowing whither they went." Robert proceeded to England. William made his headquarters at Edinburgh, where, writes his son Gilbert, " he wrought hard when he could get work, passing through a variety of difficulties."

The depressed condition of his family the poet ascribes to their having been sufferers in the cause of the Stuarts, but on this subject he is opposed by his brother Gilbert. What the poet has alleged in reference to it may be adduced in the first instance.

In his autobiographical letter to Dr Moore of 2d August 1787, the poet writes: " My ancestors rented lands off the

[1] Chambers's Life of Burns, Edinb. 1851, pp. 334, 335.

C

noble Keiths Marischal, and had the honour of sharing their
fate. I mention this because it threw my father on the
world at large. They followed boldly where their leaders led,
and welcomed ruin and shook hands with infamy, for what
they believed to be the cause of their God and their king."
In a letter to Lady Winifred Maxwell Constable, in December
1789, the poet remarks : " Though my fathers had not illustrious honours and vast properties to hazard in the contest;
though they left their humble cottages only to add so many
units more to the unnoted crowd that followed their leaders,
yet what they could they did, and what they had they lost.
With unshaken firmness, and unconcealed political attach-
ments, they shook hands with ruin for what they esteemed
the cause of their king and country." In his poetical address
to William Tytler, he refers to the subject thus:

> " My fathers that name have rever'd on a throne,
> My fathers have fallen to right it;
> Those fathers would spurn their degenerate son,
> That name should he scoffingly slight it."

It is matter of history that the poet's grandfather and
granduncle rented farms on the estate of the Earl Marischal,
the former at Clochnahill, in the parish of Dunnottar, the
latter at Elfhill, in the parish of Fetteresso. It is also certain
that the Marischal family were undeviating adherents of the
exiled house. George, tenth Earl Marischal, landlord of the
brothers Burnes, proclaimed at Aberdeen, on the 28th September 1715, at the head of his retainers, the Chevalier St
George as King of Great Britain. He commanded two squad-
rons of cavalry at the battle of Sheriffmuir, and in December
thereafter again proclaimed the Chevalier at the gate of his
house at Fetteresso. For his adherence to the Jacobite cause

he suffered attainder. That he was accompanied to Aberdeen and Sheriffmuir by his tenantry, including the brothers Burnes, is nearly certain, yet it would not appear that the latter, by enacting loyalty to their chief, sustained actual loss. They indeed possessed their farms long afterwards. From 1715 to 1721, Clochnahill farm, extending to about sixty acres, was rented for £10, 8s. 4d. sterling, and Elfhill for less than half that sum.[1] The poet's narrative cannot therefore be understood as referring to any damage sustained by his ancestors in connection with the first rebellion. In his poetical "Address to Edinburgh," he bears this retrospect:

> " Ev'n I, who sing in rustic lore,
>   Haply my sires have left their shed,
> And fac'd grim danger's loudest roar,
>   Bold following where your fathers led. "

The poet was misinformed as to the character of the support rendered to the young Chevalier at Edinburgh. Not more than three hundred of the citizens, and these of the humbler class, joined the Prince's standard.[2] Among these very probably was the poet's father. His grandfather and granduncle in Kincardineshire may also have joined the enterprise ; and this may account for the extreme poverty to which Robert Burnes was ultimately reduced. He was, we are informed by Gilbert Burns, helped by remittances from his son William. On one occasion a one pound banknote was sent, and the recipient was at a loss what to do with it, for

---

[1] There were certain minor dues. Thus the farmers at Clochnahill paid four, and the farmers at Elfhill two reikhens, or domestic fowls, which implied, according to the usage of the period, that the former tenant had four apartments, and the latter two.

[2] R. Chambers's History of the Rebellion of 1745-46, Edin. 1869, p. 162.

bank paper, as an equivalent for coin, was then scarcely known in Kincardineshire.

From Edinburgh William Burnes migrated to the neighbourhood of Ayr. The people of Ayr were zealous Presbyterians and entirely loyal, and somehow a report arose among them that the stranger had been in arms for the Chevalier. William Burnes kept pretty well his own counsel; but among his papers, according to his son Gilbert, was found a parish certificate, testifying that he had no concern "in the late wicked rebellion." This Gilbert Burns holds to be conclusive that he had not joined the army of the Prince. It is not so; the report that he had fought on the rebel side, and the poet's expressions, would induce an opposite belief. We incline to hold that William Burnes, and probably his father and uncle, bore arms in the Jacobite cause, and were among those scattered at Culloden.

Settling in the neighbourhood of Ayr, William Burnes became gardener to the laird of Fairlie, and afterwards to Mr Crawford of Doonside. At length he took a feu or perpetual lease of seven acres of land from Dr Campbell, physician in Ayr, with the view of becoming nurseryman. On his feu he built, with his own hand, a cottage of mud or clay, of which the gable fell down shortly after the birth of his first-born. Remarking his industry, Provost Ferguson of Ayr, who had lately purchased the estate of Doonholm, in the neighbourhood, induced him to abandon his nursery and become overseer of his lands. His services were so approved by Mr Ferguson, that that gentleman, with a view to improving his position, granted him the lease of a farm. The farm was styled Mount Oliphant, and consisted of about eighty acres. The rent was fixed at £40 for the first six years, and £45 thereafter. To stock the farm, Mr Ferguson gave his tenant a loan of £100. On his lease William Burnes entered at Whitsuntide 1766, and proceeded to cultivate his lands with his wonted industry. But the soil proved coarse and barren; and encountering on the death of his benefactor, Provost Ferguson, harsh usage from a merciless factor (depicted in his son's poem of the "Twa Dogs"), he, at the expiry of eleven years, quitted Mount Oliphant. At Whitsuntide 1777, he obtained the lease of Lochlea, a considerable farm in the parish of Tarbolton, and for several years he and his family enjoyed at this place a degree of comfort to which they had been strangers. But a dispute arose as to the conditions of the lease, and the matter being submitted to arbitration, William Burnes found himself by the decision a ruined man. Only a short time surviving his reverses, he died on the 13th February 1784, aged sixty-three. His remains were deposited in the churchyard of Alloway, where a simple tombstone was, by his son the poet, erected to his memory. When the poet became famous, visitors to the churchyard struck off and carried away chips from the tombstone till it wholly disappeared. It was sub-stituted by another, reared at the cost of Mr David Auld, a patriotic gentleman of the neighbourhood. The inscription was composed by the poet:

" This Stone was Erected to the
Memory of
WILLIAM BURNESS,
Late Farmer in Lochlie, Parish of Tarbolton,
Who died Feby. 13, 1784, Aged 63 years,
And was buried here.

O ye whose cheek the tear of pity stains,
Draw near with pious rev'rence and attend!
Here lie the loving Husband's dear remains,
The tender Father, and the gen'rous Friend;

> The pitying heart that felt for human woe;
>   The dauntless heart that feared no human pride;
> The friend of man, to vice alone a foe;
> ' For ev'n his failings leaned to virtue's side.' "

The eulogy is not overstrained. Tender, generous, and humane, William Burnes was beloved by his family, and venerated by his neighbours. Mr Murdoch, who taught in his house, has described him as "by far the best of the human race that he had ever the pleasure of becoming acquainted with." He adds: "He was a tender and affectionate father; he took a pleasure in leading his children in the path of virtue; not in driving them, as some parents do, to the performance of duties to which they themselves are averse. He had the art of gaining the esteem and goodwill of those that were labourers under him." In his autobiographical letter to Dr Moore, the poet has styled him irascible; but it is explained by Gilbert Burns that, having discovered the dangerous impetuosity of Robert's passions, he sought to restrain them. Mr Murdoch remarks that "he never saw him angry but twice." Reserved to strangers, he was cheerful in his household, joined his children at play, and encouraged them to regard him as their companion. To the present writer Mrs Begg spoke of her father, William Burnes, as possessed of the best qualities of mind and heart. His children, she said, admired his wisdom and revered his counsels. In his letter to Dr Moore, the poet refers to his father in these words: "After many years wanderings and sojournings, he picked up a pretty large quantity of observation and experience, to which I am indebted for most of my pretensions to wisdom. I have met," adds the poet, "with few who understood men, their manners, and their ways, equal to him."

At a period when indifference to the sacred duties was asserting itself among all ranks, William Burnes reared with becoming regularity the domestic altar. The piety of the father has, in the "Cotter's Saturday Night," been commemorated by the genius of the son.

In the form of a dialogue between father and son, William Burnes composed "A Manual of Religious Belief;" it has lately been printed as a thin octavo.[1] Evincing an intelligent appreciation of Divine truth, it is composed elegantly. The writer sets forth the leading doctrines of the Gospel, adduces evidences for the truth of Christianity, and inculcates Scripture reading as a means of informing and strengthening the moral faculty. Under the guidance of a parent so devoted and circumspect, it may not excite surprise that the poet was in youth impressed seriously.

By Mrs Begg the writer was informed that his father predicted the poet's future eminence. "Rab will one day become famous," he often said of the small boy who amused him by his lively sallies. "May he be steady, may he be virtuous," he added reverently.

In person William Burnes was above the middle height, and of slender form; he latterly stooped. He had a thoughtful and serious countenance. He married at the age of thirty-six. In the parish register of Ayr his banns of marriage are entered thus:

"Ayr, Decr. 2, 1757.—William Burns, gardener in this parish, and Agnes Broun, in Maybole, gave in their names to be proclaimed in order for marriage, and after proclamation, were married accordingly."

[1] A Manual of Religious Belief, composed by William Burnes, the Poet's father, for the instruction of his Children. Kilmarnock, 1875, 8vo, pp. 50.

The marriage was celebrated on the 15th December.[1] The bride, Agnes Broun, was born on the 17th March 1732, and was therefore in her twenty-fifth year. Her father, Gilbert Broun, farmer at Craigenton, Carrick, was thrice married, and Agnes was his eldest child by the first marriage. When she was nine years old her mother died, leaving four younger children. A sister visiting her mother on her death-bed, surprised to find her so cheerful and resigned, asked her whether she was not grieved to leave her husband and children. The dying woman replied, "I leave my children to the care of God, and Gilbert will get another wife."

Young as she was, Agnes Broun took charge of her father's younger children, for the domestic servants were chiefly employed in outdoor work. Before her mother's death she was by a country weaver taught to read the Scriptures, and at this point her education ceased. When her father contracted a second marriage, she was sent to live with her mother's mother, who told her how, in the persecuting days of her youth, she had sheltered the Covenanters.

At her grandmother's Agnes Broun used the spinning wheel in winter, and at other seasons worked in the field, sowed, reaped, and thrashed corn. She had promised her hand to her grandmother's ploughman, but after an engagement which subsisted five years, she learned that he had lapsed from virtue, and renounced him. William Burnes met her not long afterwards at Maybole fair. He had thought of proposing marriage to a young woman at Alloway Mill, but on meeting Agnes he abandoned his intention. After being courted about a year, Agnes Broun became his wife. Some-

---

[1] William Burnes's Family Bible.

what short in stature, she had a fine complexion, with pale red hair, and dark bright eyes; she was eminently cheerful, and delighted to sing the older ballads.

Though imperfectly educated, and of very ordinary capacity, Agnes Broun was a suitable helpmate to her husband. She respected his virtues, and was not insensible to his endowments. " Mrs Burnes," writes Mr Murdoch, " listened to her husband with a more marked attention than to anybody else. . . . When under the necessity of being absent, she seemed to regret as a real loss that she had missed what the good man said. She had the most marked esteem for her husband of any woman I ever knew."

Mrs Burnes survived her husband thirty-six years. For many years she resided with her son Gilbert. She died in his house at Grant's Braes, Haddingtonshire, on the 14th January 1820, in her eighty-eighth year. Her remains were deposited in Bolton churchyard, near Haddington.

Of the marriage of William Burnes and Agnes Broun were born four sons, Robert, Gilbert, William, and John; and three daughters, Agnes, Annabella, and Isabella. In the parish register of Ayr the birth of Agnes, the eldest daughter, is thus notified :—" Agnes Burns, daughter lawful of William Burns, gardener in Alloway, and Agnes Broun, his spouse, was born September 30, 1762. Baptized by Mr W. Dalrymple." She married in 1804, at Dinning, Dumfriesshire, William Galt, who became land-steward to M. Fortescue, Esq., on his estate in the north of Ireland; she died without issue, at Stephenstown, county Louth, in 1834; her remains were deposited in the churchyard of Dundalk, where a tombstone has been erected to her memory. Her husband died on the 1st March 1847.

Annabella, the second daughter, was born at Alloway on the 14th November 1764. She died, unmarried, at Grant's Braes, Haddingtonshire, on the 2d March 1832. Her remains were deposited in Bolton churchyard.

Isabella, third daughter of William Burnes and Agnes Broun, is in the Ayr register described as "lawful daughter of William Burns, farmer." Born on the 27th June 1771, she married on the 9th December 1793 John Begg, who superintended the farm of Dinning, parish of Closeburn, Dumfriesshire, rented by his brother-in-law, Gilbert Burns, and who was then non-resident, being factor at Morham Muir, Haddington. Mr John Begg subsequently became land-steward on the estate of Blackwood, Lanarkshire, belonging to Mr Hope Vere. By his horse rearing and falling upon him he was killed on the 24th April 1813.

Subsequent to her husband's death, Mrs Begg resided successively at Ormiston and Tranent till June 1843, when she settled at Bridge House, Alloway, near her birthplace. She died 4th December 1858, and her remains were consigned to the grave in Alloway churchyard, in which, seventy-five years before, her father's dust had been deposited.

Of the marriage of John Begg and Isabella Burns were born six sons, William, John, Robert Burns, Gilbert, James Hope, and Edward Hamilton; and three daughters, Agnes, Jane Breckenridge, and Isabella.

William Begg, eldest son of John Begg and Isabella Burns, was born on the 29th July 1794. In 1817 he was appointed parish schoolmaster of Ormiston, Haddingtonshire. In 1833 he resigned his office and sailed for Canada; he there resided at Clinton, Goderich, till his death, which took place on the 15th May 1864.

John Begg, second son of John Begg and Isabella Burns, was born at Mauchline on the 27th April 1796. Bred to a mechanical profession, he settled at Kilmarnock, where he died 11th October 1867. He married 14th November 1817 Agnes Wilson (born 1795, died 1851), by whom he had five sons and three daughters. John, the eldest son, born 21st March 1821, holds a farm at Pudman Creek, New South Wales; twice married, he has four sons, John, Andrew, Robert, and Neil; and a daughter, Janet.

Robert Burns Begg, second son of John Begg and Agnes Wilson, was born 9th May 1823; he married in 1846 —— Winefred, with issue. Walter Wilson, third son, born 16th July 1828, died in infancy; William, fourth son, born 1st April 1833, married in 1852, and has three sons and five daughters; James, fifth son, born 19th September 1836, died unmarried 31st May 1874.

Marion Adams Begg, eldest daughter of John Begg and Agnes Wilson, was born 17th August 1818; she married Richard Johnstone, by whom she had a son and two daughters; she died 7th February 1871. Jane Breckenridge Begg, second daughter, born 8th March 1826, married David Campbell, with issue; she and her husband reside at Largs, Ayrshire. Isabella Burns Begg, third daughter, born 27th April 1830, married George Preston; she died 3d November 1856, leaving a son and daughter.

Robert Burns Begg, third son of John Begg and Isabella Burns, was born in the parish of Dundonald, Ayrshire, and was educated at Wallace Hall Academy, Dumfriesshire. In 1818 he was appointed schoolmaster at Bent, on the estate of Blackwood; he afterwards assisted in the parish school of Dalmeny, and in 1822 was elected parish schoolmaster of

Kinross. This office he held fifty-one years. He died at Kinross on the 25th July 1876. He married, 27th July 1825, Grace, daughter of Bruce Beveridge, grand-daughter of James Beveridge, Esq. of Balado, by whom he had seven sons and three daughters.

John Begg, eldest son of Robert Burns Begg and Grace Beveridge, born 25th May 1826, is one of the owners and manager of the Kinneil Ironworks, in the county of Linlithgow. He married, first, 10th April 1855, Eliza, daughter of Andrew Vannan, distiller, Borrowstounness; and, secondly, 3d October 1865, Elizabeth Simpson, daughter of James Anderson, builder, Calcutta. He has four sons, Robert Burns, Andrew Vannan, John, and James Beveridge Anderson; also two daughters, Elizabeth Anderson, and Grace Margaret. Bruce Begg, second son of Robert Burns Begg, born 22d December 1827, died 10th December 1836. James Beveridge Begg, third son, born 24th October 1829, is settled in Virginia. He married, first, 31st August 1857, Mary Haldane ; and, secondly, 25th July 1863, Janet Haldane. He has a daughter, Mary. Robert Burns Begg, fourth son, born 1st May 1833, is a solicitor at Kinross. He married, first, 5th November 1861, Jane Hutchison; secondly, 17th March 1870, Mary Leburn, by whom he has a son, Robert Burns. Bruce Beveridge Begg, fifth son, born 24th June 1837, studied at the University of Glasgow, and in 1865 was ordained minister of Abbotshall, Fifeshire. He married, 13th December 1871, Magdalene, daughter of Andrew Currie, Esq., of Glassmount, by whom he has a son, Robert Burns, and a daughter, Elizabeth. William, sixth son, born 10th June 1839; married, 2d June 1869, Eleanor Jane Hogg. A naval engineer, he resides in Newcastle. Gilbert Burns Begg, seventh son, born 17th May 1842. A civil engineer, he resides at Motherwell, Lanarkshire. He married, 27th September 1870, Annie Cuthbertson, by whom he has a son, Robert Burns, and a daughter, Grace.

Isabella, eldest daughter of Robert Burns Begg and Grace Beveridge, was born 28th May 1831; she married, 9th August 1866, Andrew Vannan, distiller, Borrowstounness. Jane, second daughter, born 4th January 1844, died in infancy. Grace Jane, youngest daughter, born 12th February 1846, resides at Kinross, unmarried.

Gilbert Begg, fourth son of John Begg and Isabella Burns, was born on the 16th February 1802. Entering the navy, he engaged in several important services, and took part in the Crimean war. He survives, unmarried.

James Hope, fifth son of John Begg and Isabella Burns, was born on the 2d February 1809. He served in the 26th regiment, and died unmarried at Chusan, in China, 2d November 1840.

Edward Hamilton, sixth son of John Begg and Isabella Burns, born 12th August 1811, died 2d May 1824.

Jane Breckenridge, second daughter of John Begg and Isabella Burns, was born on the 16th April 1804; she died on the 7th July 1822, unmarried. Agnes Brown, the eldest daughter, born 17th April 1800, and Isabella Burns, the third daughter, born 27th April 1806, are both unmarried; they reside at Bridge House, Alloway.

John Burnes, fourth and youngest son of William Burnes and Agnes Broun, was born on the 12th July 1769. He died in his fourteenth year, and his remains were deposited in the churchyard of Mauchline.

William Burnes, third son of William Burnes and Agnes

Broun, was born at Alloway 31st July 1767. A journey-
man saddler, he prosecuted his craft, first at Newcastle,
and afterwards in London. He died at London, July 1790,
and his remains were deposited in St Paul's churchyard; the spot of his interment was unmarked, and is now
unknown.

Gilbèrt Burns, second son of William Burnes and Agnes
Broun, was born at Alloway on the 28th September 1760.
Concerning him, his early preceptor, Mr Murdoch, writes:
"Gilbert always appeared to me to possess a more lively
imagination, and to be more of the wit than Robert. . . .
Robert's countenance was generally grave, and expressive of
a serious, contemplative, and thoughtful mind. Gilbert's face
said, "*Mirth*, with thee I *mean to live;*" and certainly if any
person who knew the two boys had been asked which of them
was the most likely to court the muses, he would surely
never have guessed that Robert had a propensity of that
kind."

By ranking as a creditor of his father for his stipulated
wages on Lochlea farm, Gilbert was, in conjunction with
his brother the poet, enabled to retain a portion of farm
stock, and therewith, aided by the savings of other members
of the family, to take in lease the farm of Mossgiel, near
Mauchline. This farm was rented from Mr Gavin Hamilton,
writer in Mauchline, who himself leased the farm from the Earl
of Loudoun. In his tack, Gilbert was associated with his
brother Robert; they entered upon the farm in March 1784.
With insufficient capital, and contending with a cold, ungenerous soil, the brothers struggled hard, but the utmost
industry could not overcome the difficulties of their situation.
At length, from the proceeds of the second edition of his

poems in 1787, Robert was enabled to lend his brother the
sum of £180, which enabled him to discharge debt, and to
struggle with an ungrateful soil till 1797, when he obtained
in lease the farm of Dinning, in Nithsdale.

In 1800 Gilbert Burns was induced by Mrs Dunlop to
take temporary charge of the farm of Morham Muir, near
Haddington. His own farm at Dinning, which he retained
till 1810, Gilbert entrusted to the management of John Begg,
his sister Isabella's husband. In 1804 he accepted the
factorship of Lord Blantyre, and in the spring of that year
established his residence at Grant's Braes, near Lethington,
Haddingtonshire. In the factorship, he had in reward of
service a free house, with a salary of £100, which was subsequently advanced to £140. He died at Grant's Braes on
the 8th April 1827, aged sixty-seven. His remains were
deposited in Bolton churchyard.

Gilbert Burns facially resembled his brother the poet, with
the difference that he had an aquiline nose, the poet a
straight one. Though well-read and expert in literary composition, he devoted himself chiefly to rural affairs. To his
intelligent conversations, Dr Currie was largely indebted in
preparing the poet's memoirs. He edited an edition of his
brother's works, which was published in 1820 by Cadell and
Davies, accompanied by a dissertation from his own pen on
the effect which Presbyterianism had produced on the Scottish national character. For this edition he received from
the publishers £500, which enabled him to discharge to the
poet's widow the debt of £180 contracted thirty-two years
before. With the reserved manner of his father, he avoided
publicity, but by all to whom he was known he was respected for his worth and sagacity. Gilbert Burns married,

21st June 1791, Jean, daughter of James Breckenridge, Kilmarnock,[1] and granddaughter of James Breckenridge, parochial schoolmaster, Irvine. She was born on the 6th February 1764, and died on the 30th September 1841; her remains rest in the churchyard of Erskine, Renfrewshire.

Of the marriage of Gilbert Burns and Jean Breckenridge were born six sons and five daughters. Janet, the eldest daughter, born 23d May 1799, died 30th October 1816; Agnes, second daughter, born 16th November 1800, died 14th September 1815; Anne, third daughter, born 12th September 1805, survives; Jean, fourth daughter, born 8th June 1807, died 4th January 1827; Isabella, fifth daughter, born 17th May 1809, died 3d July 1815.

William Burns, eldest son of Gilbert Burns and Jean Breckenridge, was born on the 15th May 1792. Settling in Dublin in 1822, he married, in 1824, Jane, daughter of Peter Callanan of county Galway; she died in 1858. Of the marriage were born seven children, of whom four died young. Two sons, James and William, and a daughter, Helen, survive, all of whom are unmarried. William Burns resides at Portarlington.

James Burns, second son of Gilbert Burns, born 14th April 1794, became a writer, first at Haddington, and afterwards at Glasgow, where he was also surveyor of taxes. He latterly became factor to Lord Blantyre at Erskine, Renfrewshire, and there died 22d June 1847.

[1] Jean Breckenridge was nearly connected by marriage with Sir James Shaw, Bart., a native of Kilmarnock, Lord Mayor and Chamberlain of the city of London. Sir James became an efficient patron of the Burns family. Through his efforts the poet's three sons got a start in life. Robert, the eldest, was appointed to a post in the stamp office; James Glencairn was nominated to Christ's Hospital, where he received his education, and both he and his brother, William Nicol, obtained Indian cadetships.

Thomas Burns, third son of Gilbert Burns, was born 10th April 1796. Having studied at the University of Edinburgh, he became tutor to Sir Hew Dalrymple of North Berwick. Licensed to preach by the presbytery of Haddington on the 3d December 1822, he was on the 13th April 1826 ordained minister of Ballantrae, Ayrshire. Preferred to the living of Monkton, in the same county, he was there settled on the 18th May 1830. He joined the Free Church in 1843, and on the 25th June 1846, became minister of a Free Church congregation at Portobello, near Edinburgh. Having, along with Captain Cargill and others, projected the Free Church settlement of Otago, New Zealand, he relinquished his charge in the autumn of 1847, and with the first body of settlers sailed from Greenock as their pastor. He ministered at Otago till his death, which took place at Dunedin on the 23d January 1871. He was D.D. of the University of Edinburgh.

Dr Thomas Burns married Clementina, daughter of the Rev. James Francis Grant, rector of Merston, Sussex, son of Sir Alexander Grant of Monymusk, by whom he had one son, Arthur John, and six daughters.

Arthur John, only son of Dr Thomas Burns, married Sarah, daughter of Thomas Dickson, Otago, by whom he has had nine children. Clementina, eldest daughter of Dr Burns, married Andrew J. Elles, son of the Rev. James Elles, Saltcoats, and captain of the ship "Philip Laing," which in 1847 took out the first settlers to Otago. Of this marriage were born three sons and one daughter. James, the eldest son, is now resident at Amoy, in China; Gilbert, the second son, is settled at Oporto, and Malcolm Jamieson, the third son, resides in London. The daughter, Clementina, resides with

D

her father, who is now collector of customs at Invercargill, New Zealand.

Jane, second daughter of Dr Thomas Burns, married the Rev. William Bannerman, minister of the Presbyterian Church, Otago. They have several children.

Anne, third, and Frances, fourth daughters, married at Dunedin, Henry and Alexander, sons of —— Livingstone, formerly of Constable's publishing house, Edinburgh; both sisters have issue. Agnes, fifth daughter, is unmarried. Isabella, sixth daughter, married, at Dunedin, Alexander Stevenson. He died in 1876, leaving one son, Douglas.

Robert, fourth son of Gilbert Burns and Jean Breckenridge, was born 22d November 1797. He emigrated to South America in 1826, and there died about 1839. John, fifth son, born 6th July 1802, became a teacher of mathematics at Edinburgh, where he died 26th February 1827.

Gilbert Burns, sixth and youngest son of Gilbert Burns and Jean Breckenridge, was born at Morham Muir, Haddington-shire, 24th December 1803. Educated at the High School of Edinburgh, he entered a mercantile house, and in 1834 settled in Dublin. There he is one of the senior partners in the large mercantile house of Todd, Burns, & Co. He married in 1842, Jemima Georgiana, daughter of Alexander Ferrier of Dublin, by whom he has two sons, Robert, and Theodore Gilbert Alexander, and two daughters, Mary and Isabella.

Robert, elder son of Gilbert Burns and Jemima Ferrier, resides at the Elms, Weybridge. He married Sibylla, daughter of the Rev. Phillipps Donnithorne Dayman, vicar of Pound-stock, Cornwall, by whom he has a son, Kenneth Glencairn, and a daughter, Edith Donnithorne.

ROBERT BURNS, the poet, was the eldest son of William Burnes and Agnes Broun. His birth, in the register of Ayr parish, is recorded thus:

"Robert Burns, son law[1] to William Burns in Alloway, and Agnes Broun, his spouse, was born Jan[y] 25th 1759. Bap[d] 26th, by Mr W[m.] Dalrymple.[1] Witnesses—John Tennant[2] and James Young."

The poet was born in a clay-built cottage, which his father reared with his own hands; when he was nine days old, a portion of the gable was blown down by a gale, and the structure otherwise so shattered that he had, with his mother, to be removed to a neighbour's house. In his sixth year he was sent to a school at Alloway Mill, taught by one Campbell, but on the removal of the teacher to a post at Ayr, William Burnes and his neighbours employed a young teacher, John Murdoch, as tutor to their children. Murdoch, though

---

[1] Son of James Dalrymple, sheriff-clerk of Ayrshire, William Dalrymple was ordained to the second charge of Ayr, on the 18th December 1746 ; he was, on a vacancy, preferred to the first charge in 1756. The degree of D.D. was conferred on him by the University of St Andrews in 1779, and in 1781 he was elected moderator of the General Assembly. He died 28th January 1814, in the ninety-first year of his age, and sixty-eighth year of his ministry. Greatly reputed for his amiable dispositions and gentle manners, Dr Dalrymple is thus celebrated by Burns in "The Kirk's Alarm : "

"D'rymple, D'rymple mild,
Your heart's like a child,
And your life like the new-driven snaw."

[2] John Tennant was session-clerk of Ayr, and English master in the burgh school. It will be remarked that he enters the family name as *Burns*, such being the usual mode of spelling the name in Ayrshire. The poet, after several years spelling his name Burness, like his cousin, James Burnes of Montrose, agreed with his brother Gilbert to adopt the form used in the west of Scotland. The last time he subscribed his name "Burness" was as Deputy-Master of St James's Lodge, Tarbolton, 1st March 1786. His proposals for publishing the first or Kilmarnock edition of his poems, dated 14th April 1786, are issued in the name of *Robert Burns*.

only in his eighteenth year, was a competent instructor, and under his tuition Robert made progress in English composition. Before his ninth year he read every English book which fell in his way. At the parish school of Dalrymple and Kirkoswald he improved his handwriting, and became acquainted with geometry and land-surveying. At Ayr he studied French and the elements of Latinity. Hearing an old woman at his father's fire-side relate stories of the marvellous, he conceived a taste for poetry. His favourite poets were Ramsay and Fergusson, while he read admiringly the works of Shenstone and James Thomson. His father's straitened circumstances, while contending with the barren soil of Mount Oliphant, necessitated his working on the farm. In his fifteenth year, he on the harvest field became enamoured of a fair girl, and in her praise composed verses. He next sung of Mary Campbell, a young dairymaid, whose early death led him afterwards to compose his beautiful ode "To Mary in Heaven." Removing with his father to the farm of Lochlea, he in 1780 established at Tarbolton a literary re-union, called the Bachelor's Club. At the village of Mauchline, to which he afterwards removed, he founded another literary institution. He joined a Free Mason lodge, and became a zealous member of the craft.

On a portion of land at Lochlea he was permitted by his father to cultivate flax, and in 1781 he resolved to become a flax dresser, and so proceeded to Irvine to acquire a knowledge of the trade. But after a six month's trial his workshop was destroyed by fire, and he returned to Lochlea. His father having died in February 1784 he and his brother Gilbert rented the farm of Mossgiel, near Mauchline. During the day he worked diligently on the farm, his evenings

being devoted to literature and verse making. He courted
Jean Armour; but her father, a master mason, was opposed
to the union, and compelled her, with twin children she had
borne to the poet, to reside under his own roof. Feeling that
he had been deeply wronged, and almost driven to despair,
Burns resolved to leave the country and become a bookkeeper
at Jamaica. With this view he collected his verses, and
sending out subscription sheets, obtained for a contemplated
volume three hundred and fifty subscribers. In 1786 he
issued at Kilmarnock a thin octavo, entitled, " Poems chiefly
in the Scottish Dialect." [1] Six hundred copies were sold, and,
with the profits, amounting to twenty pounds, he paid his
passage for Jamaica, and was preparing to embark at Greenock.
Meanwhile Dr Laurie, minister of Loudoun, one of his admirers, brought his volume under the notice of Dr Blacklock
of Edinburgh, who greatly commended it, and finding the im-
pression distributed, recommended its reproduction. By the
advice of friends, Burns hastened to Edinburgh, where he
was hailed in the best literary circles. For his lodgings in
Baxter's Close, Lawnmarket, he paid a weekly rent of eighteen-
pence. He had attained the age of twenty-seven, and hitherto
his income had not exceeded seven pounds a year.

Under the patronage of the Earl of Glencairn, and other
members of the Caledonian Hunt, a second edition of his
poems was published at Edinburgh in April 1787; it was
accompanied by a list of 1500 subscribers. In May he made
a tour to the south of Scotland and into Northumberland,
visiting many interesting scenes; at Jedburgh he was presented with the freedom of the burgh. After visiting his

---

[1] The Kilmarnock edition was published at 3s.; a copy sold recently by
auction for £60.

relations at Mossgiel in June, he returned to Edinburgh, and from thence proceeded to Dunfermline, there to inspect the grave of King Robert the Bruce. In September he made an excursion to Stirling and the Highlands. Among those who extended to him special hospitalities were, Sir William Murray at Ochtertyre, the Duke of Athole at Blair Athole, and the Duke of Gordon at Gordon Castle.

Returning to Edinburgh, the poet celebrated the birthday of Prince Charles Edward on the last day of December, and on the occasion produced an ode, breathing Jacobite sentiments. In the Canongate churchyard he traced the grave of the poet, Robert Fergusson, and at the spot reared a tombstone to his memory. While at Edinburgh he conducted his celebrated correspondence with "Clarinda," the accomplished Mrs M'Lehose.

Having sold the copyright of his poems to Mr Creech for £100, he left Edinburgh in the summer of 1788 possessed of nearly £500. To his brother Gilbert he gave a loan of £180, and with the balance stocked the farm of Ellisland, in Nithsdale, which he obtained in lease from Mr Miller of Dalswinton, one of his admirers. Through his friend, Mr Graham of Fintry, he was appointed Excise officer of the district surrounding his farm. As a farmer he did not prosper, and renouncing his lease in 1791, he established his residence at Dumfries as an officer of Excise; his salary was not more than £70.

He continued to invoke the muse. To Johnson's "Musical Museum" he contributed 190 songs, original and amended; he also furnished words to numerous airs in Mr George Thomson's "Collection."

At Dumfries his society was cherished, while many notable

persons at a distance sought his correspondence. Unhappily he did not always prefer the companionship of persons worthy of his genius; and while he never neglected his professional duties, he indulged in social pleasures somewhat too freely. Keenly advocating political progress, he sympathised with the principles of the French Convention; but when licentiousness usurped the place of patriotism, and British liberties came to be endangered, he stood firmly by the Constitution, and became a volunteer.

Though possessing a well-knit frame, Burns was not robust. In early manhood he suffered from an imperfect circulation, and was subject to nocturnal attacks of palpitation and faintness. On account of his political opinions, he incurred some disapproval, and in moments of depression he fancied that he was the victim of detraction. In the spring of 1795 his health became feeble, and the death of an infant daughter in the following autumn, accelerated his complaint. He was attacked with rheumatic fever, and having before his recovery exposed himself at a convivial party, he contracted a serious illness. Sea-bathing, to which he had recourse, did not prove remedial. On the 21st July 1796 he breathed his last.

Burns died at the early age of thirty-seven. Ten years before his death he was unknown out of his own neighbourhood. Misfortune drove him into print, and what he printed charmed and electrified his countrymen. At once he became famous; he was *fêted* in the capital, men of letters courted his society, and persons of noble rank admitted him to intimacy. As a household word his name flashed over Scotland. Long before his death his poems were read and his songs lilted in every Highland vale and Lowland hamlet. The elder minstrelsy with its impurities was rejected, and in

its stead his verses were accepted everywhere. He had caught
the lispings of nature and made them vocal. In his verses the
humblest peasant caught the glow of patriotism and the spirit
of independence. He was the greatest Scotsman of his century.

Illustrious as he was, Burns had failings incident to huma-
nity. Descended paternally from a Celtic stock, he was in-
fluenced by the passionate fervour of that impressible race.
Somewhat too prone to share the pleasures of society, he contracted habits which were injurious to him. But, sun-like, his
genius rose above the clouds which threatened to obscure it.
He was, as his sister Mrs Begg informed the writer, a sincere
believer in the Christian verities; he discharged the duties of
the family altar after his father's death, and was careful that
his younger sister should be instructed in the church cate-
chism. He regretted his errors, actively fulfilled the duties of
his office, lived within the bounds of his income, and died
without debt.

In person the poet was nearly five feet nine inches in
height; he was well formed but stooped slightly. His face
was of the dark Celtic type, with features strongly marked;
he had a straight nose, and penetrating dark eyes, deeply set.
"His countenance so beamed with genius," remarked to the
writer, his sister, Mrs Begg, "that any one seeing him even
incidentally was not likely to forget him." His head was
large, but in the upper part flat rather than arched; his fore-
head was broad, but not high. Unobtrusive in society, he
impressed all who listened to him when he entered heartily
into conversation.

On Monday the 25th July 1796, being four days after his
death, his remains were interred in St Michael's churchyard,
Dumfries. On the evening of the preceding day the body

was placed in the Town Hall, where it lay in state till the time of burial. The Dumfriesshire Volunteers determined that their illustrious comrade should be buried with military honours. The Angusshire Fencibles and the Cinque Ports Cavalry, then stationed in the place, offered assistance. Among the junior officers of the latter was Mr Jenkinson, afterwards Earl of Liverpool and Prime Minister. Ten thousand persons joined the funeral procession.

The bard's remains were deposited in a spot in the northeast corner of the churchyard, which some years previously he had purchased. There a plain tombstone bearing the date of his death was erected by his widow. In 1815 an elegant mausoleum in honour of his memory was by public subscription raised in St Michael's churchyard, to the vault under which his remains were reverently transferred on the 19th September of that year. The mausoleum is in the form of a Greek temple; it is adorned with a mural sculpture by Turnerelli, representing the Genius of Scotland finding Burns at the plough, and casting over him her poetic mantle. In 1784 the poet met Jean Armour, who afterwards became his wife. Born 27th February 1765 [1] she was one of the eleven children of James Armour, master mason, residing in the Cowgate of Mauchline. From his wife in disposition and habits James Armour essentially differed. A model of industry, he steadily laboured at his craft, and in private life was sober, earnest, and circumspect. Mrs Armour lacked diligence, and herself attached to frivolous pastimes, she encouraged similar tastes in her children. In one respect

[1] The year 1765 is the date on the gravestone in the mausoleum in St Michael's churchyard. It was the original entry also in the poet's family Bible, but it has been erased, and the year 1767 substituted.

only did her daughters profit by her example; they contracted a taste for music. Jean Armour sung sweetly, and this accomplishment, in addition to her personal charms, won the poet's love. He celebrated her in song, and early in 1786 privately owned her as his wife. But her father opposed the union, and the poet experienced an irregular divorce. James Armour afterwards relented, and in 1788 allowed his daughter to join her husband.

Mrs Burns died at Dumfries on the 26th March 1834 in the same house in which the poet expired thirty-eight years previously. Through the profits of her husband's works, certain private benefactions, and latterly by the generosity of her sons, she was comfortably maintained.

By his wife, Jean Armour, the poet was father of five sons and four daughters. Jean, the eldest daughter, a twin with her brother Robert, was born on the 3d September 1786; she died at the age of fourteen months. Twin daughters, born on the 3d March 1788, died soon after birth. Elizabeth Riddel, the youngest daughter, so named in honour of Mrs Riddel of Glenriddel, was born on the 21st November 1792; she died at Mauchline in the autumn of 1795, and was there buried. The poet, whose health was already broken, was too ill to attend her funeral.

Of the poet's five sons, Francis Wallace, the second son, so named in honour of Mrs Dunlop of Dunlop, was born on the 18th August 1789; he died 9th July 1803, at the age of fourteen. Maxwell, the fifth and youngest son, named after Dr Maxwell, the physician who attended the poet in his last illness, was born 26th July 1796 (the day of his father's funeral); he died 24th April 1799, aged two years and nine months.

Robert Burns, the poet's eldest son, a twin with his sister Jean, was born 3d September 1786. From the grammar school of Dumfries, he proceeded to the University of Edinburgh, where he studied during two sessions. Another session he spent at the University of Glasgow. Having procured an appointment in the Stamp Office, he entered on his duties at London in 1804. In 1833 he got his superannuation allowance, when he visited his mother at Dumfries, whom he had not seen for twenty-six years. At Dumfries he fixed his residence. There in the summer of 1856 the writer of these Memoirs paid him a visit. Being ten years old when his father died he remembered him, but not so as to describe his personal aspects. Into the hands of his son the bard placed the works of the English poets, and encouraged him to read them, which he did. But he never spoke of his own verses; nor did the son know that his father was a poet until the neighbours, after his decease, spoke of him as such to his mother. In form of cranium and facial lineaments Robert strongly resembled his father. With a vigorous intellect, improved by extensive and varied reading, he possessed a memory singularly retentive. In London he added to his finances by giving instruction in mathematics and in the classics. He excelled in conversation. He died on the 14th May 1857, at the age of seventy-one; his remains were conveyed to the vault of his father's mausoleum. He married at London, on the 24th March 1809, Anne Sherwood, by whom he had a daughter Eliza, who married, on the 27th September 1836, Bartholomew James Everitt, assistant-surgeon in the East India Company's service, who died at London on the 20th April 1840.

The only child of Mr and Mrs Everitt, Martha Burns

Everitt, is unmarried. Mrs Everitt resides at Bathwick Hill, Bath.

William Nicol Burns, third son of the poet, was born at Ellisland on the 9th April 1791; he was named in honour of his father's friend, William Nicol, of Edinburgh. Educated at Dumfries Academy, he in his sixteenth year sailed to India as a midshipman. Not long afterwards he obtained an Indian cadetship. Proceeding to the Madras Presidency, he there served as an officer of the 7th Native Infantry for thirty-three years. He ultimately commanded his regiment. In 1843 he retired from the army, and returning to Britain settled at Cheltenham with his brother, James Glencairn, then Major Burns. In 1855 he became colonel by brevet. He died at Cheltenham on the 21st February 1872, aged eighty-one. His remains were deposited in the vault of the poet's mausoleum. He married in 1822 Catherine Adelaide, daughter of Richard Crone, of Summer Hill, Dublin, who died, without issue, at Killudghee, in India, on the 29th June 1841.

James Glencairn Burns, the poet's fourth son, was born at Dumfries on the 12th August 1794, and was named after his father's friend, James, Earl of Glencairn. He was educated at Dumfries Academy and Christ's Hospital, London. Obtaining a cadetship, he sailed for India in June 1811. Arriving at Calcutta, he there joined the 15th Regiment of Bengal Native Infantry. In 1817 he was appointed by the Marquis of Hastings, Governor-General, to an important post in the Commissariat. As Captain Burns, he visited Britain in 1831, returning to India in 1833, when he received from Lord Metcalfe the important office of Judge and Collector of Cachar. In 1839 he finally returned to Britain with the rank of major. For several years he resided near London.

He acted as Government Commissioner in an inquiry into the condition of the operatives in paper mills, on which he presented a valuable report. His brother, Lieutenant-Colonel William Nicol Burns, having retired from active service in 1843, he arranged to reside with him in Cheltenham. In 1844 the brothers were celebrated by a festive "Welcome" on the banks of the Doon. James Glencairn Burns obtained the brevet rank of Lieutenant-Colonel in 1855. He died at Cheltenham on the 18th November 1865, and his remains were consigned to the vault of the poet's mausoleum.

With the Colonels Burns, the writer of these Memoirs possessed considerable intimacy. Colonel William Burns was an amiable, kindly man; he had the same type of face, but otherwise did not resemble his father. Colonel James was an accomplished Oriental scholar; he was occasionally chosen examiner in Hindustanee, in Cheltenham College. Possessed of dramatic power, he took part in private theatricals. He inherited a rheumatic tendency, which, he remarked to the writer, had afflicted him from childhood. Abundantly facetious and good-humoured, he nevertheless keenly resented any ungenerous reflection on his father's memory.

Colonel James Glencairn Burns married first, in April 1818, Sarah, daughter of James Robinson of Sunderland, who died at Neemuch, in India, on the 7th November 1821, at the age of twenty-four. Of their marriage were born a son, Robert Shaw, who died in India, on the 11th December 1821, aged eighteen months; also two daughters, of whom one, Jean Isabella, died at sea, 5th June 1823, in her fifth year.

Sarah, the surviving daughter, born 2d November 1821, married at Cheltenham on the 24th July 1847, Dr Berkeley Westropp Hutchinson, a native of Galway, by whom she has had a son, Robert Burns, and three daughters, Annie, Violet Burns, and Margaret Constance Burns.

Robert Burns Hutchinson, only son of Dr Berkeley Hutchinson and Sarah Burns, was educated at Christ's Hospital, London. In 1877 he sailed for Assam, there to engage in business as a tea planter. He is the only male descendant of the poet now living.

Colonel James Burns married, secondly, in June 1828, Mary, daughter of Captain Beckett of Enfield; she died at Gravesend, 13th November 1844, aged fifty-two. Her only child, Annie Beckett, born 7th September 1830, resides at Cheltenham, unmarried.

The armorial bearings of the family of Burnes, granted to Dr James Burnes, K.H., and other descendants of his paternal grandfather, are in the Lyon register recorded thus:

"*Arms.*—Ermine, on a bend azure, an escocheon, or, charged

with a hollybush, surmounted by a crook and bugle horn

saltyreways, all proper, being the device of the poet Burns and on a chief gules, the White Horse of Hanover, between two Eastern crowns, or, in allusion to the Guelphic Order, conferred on James Burnes, K.H., by King William IV., and to the distinguished services of him and his brothers in India.

"*Crests.*—On the dexter side, one of augmentation, in allusion to the devotion to their country, shown by the late Lieut.-Colonel Sir Alexander Burnes, C.B., and Lieutenant Charles Burnes. Out of a mural crown, per pale, vert, and gules, the rim inscribed "Cabool," in letters argent, a demi-eagle displayed, transfixed by a javelin in bend sinister proper; on the sinister, that previously borne, viz.: Issuant from an Eastern crown or, an oak tree shivered, renewing its foliage proper.

"*Motto.*—Ob Patriam Vulnera Passi."

INDEX.

E

M'Farlane & Erskine, Printers, Edinburgh.

www.ingramcontent.com/pod-product-compliance
Lightning Source LLC
Chambersburg PA
CBHW060633280326
41933CB00012B/2023